# The Exploring The Let Them Grow Method

## A Simple Tool That's Transforming Lives Everywhere

Alexander doe

# Table of content

# 7. Creating a Legacy of Growth for the Future

## Chapter 1: The Power of Letting Growth Happen

Growth is a process that transcends time, experience, and effort. It isn't something we can force, rush, or control. It is something that unfolds naturally when we create the right conditions for it to happen. This chapter focuses on the profound impact of allowing growth to happen, both in ourselves and in others.

At its core, growth is about change. It's the evolution of our thoughts, emotions, behaviors, and beliefs over time. Sometimes, we think that growth requires constant pushing, endless striving, or rigid discipline. While these things can play a role in the process, they are not the driving forces. The driving force behind real, lasting growth is allowing it to happen in its own time and space.

This idea is counterintuitive for many. We live in a society that celebrates constant activity, measurable results, and immediate success. We're told to act fast, grow quickly, and achieve more with less. This mindset, however, can be detrimental to the natural flow of growth.

**The Illusion of Control**

The first step in understanding the power of letting growth happen is acknowledging the illusion of control. We often believe that by exerting control over a situation or a person, we can push growth forward. But growth doesn't work that way. When we focus too much on controlling outcomes, we actually stifle growth by creating stress, pressure, and expectations.

Think about a garden. A gardener doesn't try to control the growth of the plants in a garden. They provide the right environment — the soil, the water, the sunlight — and then step back. The plants grow at their own pace. The gardener trusts that, given the right conditions, the plants will grow naturally. This same principle applies to our own growth and the growth of others. We need to create the right conditions and then trust that growth will occur on its own.

**Creating the Right Conditions for Growth**

Letting growth happen starts with creating the right environment for it. This environment can be physical, emotional, or mental. In our personal lives, this means creating a space where we feel safe, valued, and supported. We need to surround ourselves with people who encourage our growth, challenge us in positive ways, and allow us to evolve without judgment.

It also means giving ourselves permission to fail, to make mistakes, and to learn from those mistakes. Growth isn't linear. It doesn't follow a predictable path, and it doesn't happen all at once. By embracing the process, we allow ourselves to grow in a way that feels natural and sustainable.

The environment also includes the mental space we cultivate for ourselves. This is where mindset comes into play. To let growth happen, we must adopt a mindset that is open to learning, open to change, and open to possibility. This is not always easy, especially when we face challenges, setbacks, or uncertainty. But a mindset that is grounded in the belief that growth will come with time and effort is essential for fostering an environment where growth can thrive.

**The Power of Patience**

Patience is one of the most important qualities in letting growth happen. When we are patient, we acknowledge that growth takes time. It cannot be rushed, and it cannot be forced. For example, consider a child learning to walk. The child doesn't wake up one day and starts walking immediately. The process involves trial and error, falling and getting up again, trying new movements, and learning from each attempt. The child doesn't rush the process.

Instead, they trust that, with time, they will learn to walk.

Similarly, we must trust the process of growth. Whether it's personal development, professional achievement, or relationships, growth takes time. There will be setbacks, moments of doubt, and times when it feels like we're not making progress. But patience allows us to remain steady in the face of adversity. It allows us to continue moving forward, even when it feels slow.

**Letting Go of Perfection**

One of the biggest obstacles to allowing growth is our attachment to perfection. Many of us are conditioned to believe that growth is only valuable if it's perfect, if we're constantly improving, or if we're achieving success at every step. This mindset can be incredibly limiting. Perfectionism often paralyzes us from taking action, from stepping into new opportunities, or from allowing ourselves to be vulnerable.

Letting go of the need to be perfect is a powerful step in allowing growth to happen. It gives us the freedom to fail, to make mistakes, and to learn from those experiences. It allows us to embrace our imperfections and see them as part of the growth process. In fact, many of our most important lessons come from the times when we've stumbled, faltered, or faced challenges.

Perfectionism often prevents us from seeing the beauty in imperfection. The most extraordinary growth happens when we're willing to embrace our flaws, our mistakes, and our struggles. It's in these moments that we learn the most about ourselves and our capacity to change.

**Trusting the Process**

Trust is at the heart of allowing growth to happen. It's the trust that we are on the right path, even when we don't have all the answers. It's the trust that, even when things don't go according to plan, we are still learning, still evolving, and still growing.

When we trust the process, we let go of the need for immediate results or validation. We stop measuring our progress by external standards and start measuring it by our own internal growth. This shift in perspective allows us to relax, to be present in the moment, and to trust that growth is happening, even if we can't always see it.

### The Ripple Effect of Growth

The power of letting growth happen extends beyond ourselves. When we allow ourselves to grow, we inspire others to do the same. Our growth creates a ripple effect that influences those around us. This is especially true in relationships. When we model patience, trust, and acceptance in our relationships, we create an environment where others feel safe to grow as well.

This is the beauty of the Let Them Grow Method. It's not just about our own growth.

It's about creating a culture of growth, where everyone is encouraged to evolve and become the best versions of themselves. Whether in our families, friendships, workplaces, or communities, the power of letting growth happen has the potential to change lives.

**Conclusion**

The power of letting growth happen lies in our willingness to surrender control, trust the process, and create the right environment for growth to unfold. Growth is a natural, ongoing process that doesn't need to be forced or rushed. By embracing patience, letting go of perfection, and trusting the journey, we allow ourselves to grow in a way that is sustainable, meaningful, and transformative.

As you reflect on this chapter, think about areas of your life where you might be trying to control the process of growth. Are there places where you are pushing too hard or expecting immediate results? How can you create the right environment for growth to happen more naturally? By answering these questions, you'll begin to open up space for real, lasting growth in your life.

## Chapter 2: Understanding the Roots of Growth

Growth is a deeply rooted process, just like a tree that starts as a seed and slowly spreads its roots deep into the earth. To truly understand growth, we need to examine its roots — the fundamental elements that make growth possible. In this chapter, we will explore the underlying principles that drive growth and how recognizing these roots can help you foster growth in every area of your life.

### The Seed of Potential

Every form of growth starts with a seed. It could be an idea, a goal, a dream, or a desire for change. Much like a seed, growth begins small. It's easy to overlook or underestimate its potential at the beginning. However, the seed holds everything necessary for the plant — or in this case, growth — to flourish.

The seed represents your potential. It's the spark of possibility within you, the first glimmer of change. But for that seed to grow, it must be nurtured. It needs the right conditions, the right environment, and the right amount of time. Without these factors, the seed will struggle to grow or might even wither away. But when nurtured properly, the seed will sprout, grow roots, and develop into something beautiful and strong.

Likewise, in our lives, growth begins with a vision — a seed of possibility. Whether it's a personal transformation, the development of a skill, or a shift in our mindset, growth always starts small. The key is to recognize that potential and give it the room it needs to expand.

### The Role of Environment

Once the seed is planted, the next critical factor is its environment. A tree's roots spread out in search of water, nutrients, and stability. Similarly, the environment you create for your growth can either support or hinder your progress.

Think about your own life. What environment are you creating for your personal growth? Are you surrounded by people who support you, encourage you, and help you push forward? Or are you in an environment that challenges you in unhealthy ways, creating stress and self-doubt? Just like a plant needs sunlight, water, and good soil to thrive, you need the right support system, positive influences, and the right mindset to fuel your growth.

In addition to the people around you, the physical environment matters too. The spaces you inhabit, whether it's your home, your workplace, or your social spaces, influence your mindset and energy. A cluttered or toxic environment can stunt growth, while a positive, calm, and supportive space can encourage it. Ask yourself: What elements in my environment are either fostering or limiting my growth?

**Internal Conditions for Growth**

While the external environment is important, the internal environment plays an equally crucial role in growth. The way we think, feel, and perceive the world around us determines how we approach challenges and opportunities. Without a strong inner environment, even the most supportive external conditions can fall short.

Our inner environment consists of our beliefs, attitudes, and emotional state. A mindset rooted in fear, doubt, and negativity can prevent growth, even if all the external conditions are perfect. On the other hand, a mindset of openness, curiosity, and optimism creates fertile ground for growth to happen.

To cultivate this inner environment, we need to be mindful of the thoughts we entertain and the emotions we allow to take root. Just as we would pull out weeds from a garden to protect the plants, we need to uproot limiting beliefs and negative thoughts that stifle our growth. This process takes time and effort, but the payoff is immense.

### The Power of Patience in the Early Stages

When you plant a seed, you don't see the results immediately. You don't see the roots growing under the soil or the tiny shoots pushing through the earth. Growth is often invisible at first, happening beneath the surface. The same is true for personal growth. In the early stages, the changes you're experiencing may not be immediately visible. It may feel like nothing is happening, even though growth is taking place in ways you can't yet see.

This is where patience becomes crucial. Just like a seed needs time to grow its roots before it can sprout, your growth requires time to develop and expand. It's easy to become frustrated when we don't see immediate results, but trust in the process. The roots are forming, even if they're not visible yet.

Allowing yourself to be patient in this phase is key to long-term success. It can be tempting to rush the process, to push for faster results, or to force growth when it doesn't seem to be happening on our timeline. However, growth takes its own time, and forcing it can lead to burnout or stagnation. Instead, practice patience and trust that, in time, the changes you're making will surface in meaningful ways.

**Understanding the Role of Resistance**

When growth begins, it's not always smooth sailing. There will be resistance — internal and external — that will challenge your progress. Resistance might come in the form of self-doubt, fear of failure, or external obstacles that seem to block your path. While resistance can feel discouraging, it is actually a natural and necessary part of the growth process.

Consider how a plant must push through the soil to reach the surface. The soil may be dense, the conditions may be tough, and there may be barriers in the way, but the plant's instinct is to push through. In the same way, resistance helps strengthen your growth. It challenges you to develop resilience, problem-solving skills, and the ability to adapt.

Resistance is not something to avoid; it's something to embrace. Each challenge you encounter in the process of growth is an opportunity to develop your strength and deepen your understanding. The key is not to fight resistance but to work with it — to use it as a catalyst for further development.

**Nourishing Growth with Positive Energy**

Once the roots of growth are established, they need to be nourished. Positive energy acts as the water, sunlight, and nutrients that keep growth thriving. Positive energy comes from a variety of sources, including self-love, gratitude, encouragement from others, and a sense of purpose.

Just as a tree needs consistent care to continue growing strong, your growth requires ongoing nourishment. This nourishment might come in the form of positive affirmations, moments of reflection, or acts of kindness. Surround yourself with positive influences and practices that uplift you and keep you motivated on your growth journey.

It's also important to stay connected to your "why" — the reason you want to grow in the first place. When you are connected to your purpose, growth becomes easier because it's aligned with your deepest desires. Nourish your growth with positive energy and a clear sense of purpose.

**Conclusion**

Understanding the roots of growth is essential for creating a life of lasting change. Growth doesn't happen overnight, and it doesn't happen without effort. It begins with the seed of potential, thrives in a supportive environment, and is nurtured by patience, resilience, and positive energy.

As you reflect on this chapter, think about your own growth journey. What are the roots that have already taken hold in your life? What are the conditions that you need to cultivate in order to support your growth moving forward? By answering these questions, you can better understand the foundational elements that will drive your growth and help you create a sustainable path toward fulfillment.

## Chapter 3: Letting Go to Allow Room for Growth

Growth, in any aspect of life, is not simply about adding new things. Often, it's about creating space for the new by letting go of what no longer serves us. Letting go is a key element of the Let Them Grow Method, and in this chapter, we will explore why letting go is essential for growth and how you can make this practice part of your daily life.

### The Importance of Space in Growth

When you plant a seed, it needs space to spread its roots and grow. If the soil is compacted or overcrowded, the seed will struggle to grow properly. In the same way, when we are bogged down by unnecessary baggage — whether it's past experiences, limiting beliefs, or unhealthy attachments — we create internal and external barriers that prevent us from flourishing.

Letting go is about making room for new possibilities, new opportunities, and new energy. Without this space, growth becomes stifled. Imagine trying to fill a glass that's already full; no matter how much water you pour in, it will spill over. Similarly, if your mind and life are already filled with clutter — emotional, mental, or physical — there's no room for growth to take root.

This is why letting go is a vital part of the growth process. It's not about giving up or abandoning your past. It's about creating the room you need to evolve, to stretch, and to move forward with greater clarity and purpose.

**Letting Go of Limiting Beliefs**

One of the most significant obstacles to growth is limiting beliefs. These are the thoughts we hold about ourselves, our abilities, and our potential that limit what we believe is possible. Examples of limiting beliefs include thoughts like, "I'm not good enough," "I can't change," or "I don't deserve success." These beliefs act as barriers, blocking the flow of growth in our lives.

To allow for growth, it's essential to identify and challenge these limiting beliefs. Ask yourself: What beliefs do I hold about myself that may be limiting my potential? How can I begin to shift these beliefs to align with the person I want to become?

Letting go of limiting beliefs requires self-awareness and courage. It means facing the fears and doubts that have been holding you back and choosing to replace them with empowering beliefs. For example, instead of believing "I can't succeed," replace it with "I am capable of growth and learning." This shift may not happen overnight, but each step you take toward letting go of limiting beliefs creates space for new, empowering beliefs to take root.

### Releasing Attachments to the Past

Another crucial aspect of letting go is releasing attachments to the past. We often hold onto past experiences, whether they are failures, regrets, or unresolved emotional wounds, because we believe they define us. However, this attachment to the past can prevent us from moving forward and embracing new possibilities.

Consider a plant growing in the soil. If it constantly held onto the old leaves that had already fallen off, it wouldn't be able to make room for new growth. Similarly, holding onto past pain, resentment, or regret can prevent us from flourishing in the present. To grow, we must release our attachment to the past and allow ourselves to fully experience the present moment.

This doesn't mean forgetting the past or denying its importance. It simply means not letting it control our present or future. Releasing attachment to the past allows us to embrace new opportunities and experiences without the weight of old stories or patterns.

**Letting Go of Control**

Control is another major barrier to growth. We often try to control every aspect of our lives, from how others behave to the outcomes of our efforts. But growth doesn't happen when we force it. In fact, the need for control can often prevent growth by creating anxiety, resistance, and rigid expectations.

The truth is, control is an illusion. We cannot control everything, and in trying to do so, we close ourselves off to the natural flow of life. Growth requires us to let go of the need to control and instead trust the process. It means surrendering to the flow of life and being open to whatever comes our way, knowing that each experience, whether it's a success or failure, is an opportunity for growth.

Letting go of control doesn't mean being passive or careless. It means letting go of the attachment to specific outcomes and embracing the journey of growth itself. Trusting the process allows you to remain flexible and open to the many ways in which growth can unfold in your life.

**Releasing Fear and Doubt**

Fear and doubt are some of the most powerful forces that prevent us from letting go and allowing growth to happen. When we fear the unknown or doubt our abilities, we are less likely to take the necessary risks that lead to growth. Fear keeps us stuck in our comfort zones, where there is little room for expansion.

To create room for growth, we must face our fears and doubts head-on. This doesn't mean eliminating fear altogether, but rather learning to work with it. Fear is a natural part of the growth process; it's a sign that we are stepping outside of our comfort zone and moving into new territory. Instead of letting fear control us, we can use it as a signal to take bold action.

One way to release fear is through mindfulness. By becoming aware of your fears and acknowledging them without judgment, you can create space between you and the fear itself. This space allows you to respond to fear with courage and clarity, rather than reacting from a place of panic or avoidance.

**The Art of Letting Go in Relationships**

In relationships, letting go can be particularly challenging. We may feel a strong attachment to certain people, ideas, or expectations, and we may fear that letting go will lead to loss or disconnection. However, letting go is essential for the health and growth of relationships.

Letting go in relationships means releasing the need to control others, to fix them, or to impose your own expectations on them. It means allowing others to be who they are and giving them the freedom to grow in their own way. When we let go of control in relationships, we create a space for true connection and mutual respect.

In romantic relationships, friendships, or family dynamics, letting go allows both individuals to thrive as individuals, which in turn strengthens the relationship. It's about finding a balance between support and independence, nurturing the growth of both people without stifling each other.

**Creating Space for New Opportunities**

Finally, letting go allows you to create space for new opportunities. When we hold on to old habits, mindsets, or situations, we block the flow of new experiences. Letting go is an invitation to release the old and welcome the new.

In your personal and professional life, releasing the old opens up space for fresh ideas, new relationships, and exciting possibilities. Whether it's letting go of a job that no longer aligns with your values or releasing outdated goals that no longer inspire you, each act of letting go creates space for new opportunities to enter your life.

## Conclusion

Letting go is not a passive act; it is an empowering practice that allows growth to unfold naturally. By letting go of limiting beliefs, attachments to the past, the need for control, and fear, you create space for new possibilities. This space enables you to grow, not just in one area of life, but in all areas.

As you reflect on this chapter, consider what you need to let go of in your own life. What beliefs, fears, or attachments are holding you back from experiencing growth? How can you begin to release them to make room for the new? By practicing the art of letting go, you will allow yourself to step into a future filled with endless potential.

## Chapter 4: The Role of Patience in the Growing Process

Growth, whether personal, professional, or in relationships, is rarely instantaneous. In our fast-paced world, we often want immediate results, but growth is a process that requires time, attention, and patience. The Let Them Grow Method emphasizes the importance of patience in allowing both ourselves and others to evolve naturally. In this chapter, we will explore why patience is a vital component of growth and how you can develop it as part of your journey.

### Why Patience is Key to Growth

Growth is not something that can be rushed. It is a gradual process that requires nurturing, understanding, and time. Whether you're working to develop a new skill, build a relationship, or create personal transformation, growth takes time to unfold. Patience is the recognition that growth is an ongoing journey rather than a destination.

When you are patient with the process of growth, you allow it to happen naturally, without forcing or rushing the outcomes. Think of it like planting a tree. You wouldn't expect it to bear fruit overnight; it takes time to grow deep roots, expand its branches, and reach its full potential. Similarly, when you approach personal or professional growth with patience, you give yourself the opportunity to grow into the person you are meant to be.

Patience also allows you to approach setbacks with a sense of calm. Instead of getting discouraged or frustrated when things don't go as planned, you learn to trust the process, knowing that the difficulties you face are part of the growth journey. As you develop patience, you cultivate resilience — the ability to keep going even when progress feels slow or uncertain.

**The Dangers of Rushing Growth**

In our modern society, there is a tendency to rush the process of growth. We are constantly bombarded with messages that tell us to work harder, achieve faster, and produce quicker results. While this may work in some situations, it is detrimental to growth in many areas of life.

When we rush growth, we bypass important lessons and experiences that are necessary for deep transformation. Think about how hurrying the growing process of a plant might lead to its premature death. Similarly, rushing your own growth can result in shallow, unsustainable changes. Without giving yourself the necessary time to integrate the lessons you learn, you might miss important insights and end up back where you started.

Rushing can also lead to burnout. If you push yourself too hard or set unrealistic expectations, you risk overwhelming yourself and derailing your progress. Growth needs time to breathe, and trying to rush it can lead to exhaustion and disappointment. Instead of trying to force things to happen, patience allows you to remain consistent and steady in your efforts, which ultimately leads to more lasting and meaningful growth.

**Patience and Self-Compassion**

Patience isn't just about waiting; it's about being kind and compassionate to yourself while you wait. Often, when we feel like we're not making progress fast enough, we can become our own harshest critics. We set impossible standards for ourselves and beat ourselves up when we fall short. This lack of self-compassion can undermine our growth process, creating stress and anxiety that make it harder to progress.

To cultivate patience, it's essential to practice self-compassion. This means acknowledging that growth is a journey, and like any journey, it comes with its challenges. Instead of criticizing yourself for not being where you want to be, practice patience by treating yourself with kindness and understanding. Celebrate your small wins, be gentle with your mistakes, and remember that every step, no matter how small, is progress.

When you are compassionate with yourself, you allow growth to happen without unnecessary pressure or self-imposed deadlines. You understand that growth is not linear and that setbacks are simply opportunities to learn and evolve. Self-compassion creates an environment where patience can thrive, and growth can take root without the constant fear of falling behind.

### Cultivating Patience in Daily Life

Patience is a skill that can be developed through practice. It's not something that comes easily to everyone, especially in a world where instant gratification is the norm. However, with consistent effort, you can learn to cultivate patience in all areas of your life. Here are some ways you can practice patience daily:

1. **Mindfulness**: Practicing mindfulness helps you become more aware of your thoughts and emotions in the present moment. It allows you to observe your impatience without letting it control you. By being mindful, you can choose to respond to impatience with calmness and clarity instead of frustration.

2. **Setting Realistic Expectations**: One of the key reasons we struggle with impatience is because we set unrealistic expectations for ourselves and others. When you expect rapid results or perfection, it's easy to become frustrated when things don't go as planned. Instead, set realistic expectations that align with the natural process of growth. Understand that growth takes time and that mistakes and setbacks are part of the journey.

3. **Focusing on the Process**: Instead of fixating on the end result, shift your

focus to the process itself. Growth is not just about the destination; it's about the lessons you learn along the way. By focusing on the process, you can enjoy the journey of growth and find meaning in each step you take.

4. **Practicing Gratitude**: Gratitude helps you appreciate the progress you've made, even if it's not as fast as you'd like. By acknowledging what you've accomplished so far, you create a positive mindset that allows you to be patient with the rest of your journey. Gratitude shifts your focus away from what you don't have to what you already have, which cultivates patience and contentment.

5. **Embracing the Slow Pace**: Sometimes, the best way to develop patience is to simply embrace the slow pace of growth. Take time to savor the small moments, and trust that even the slowest progress is still progress. Rather than rushing through tasks or

achievements, allow yourself to experience the present moment fully, knowing that growth is happening at its own pace.

**Patience in Relationships**

In relationships, patience is often the key to building strong, lasting connections. Whether it's with family, friends, or romantic partners, patience allows you to truly understand and accept others as they are, without rushing them to change or meet your expectations.

When we are patient in our relationships, we give others the space they need to grow at their own pace. We stop trying to fix them, and instead, we support them in their personal growth journeys. This creates an environment of trust and understanding, where both individuals can evolve naturally and authentically.

Patience in relationships also helps us navigate challenges more effectively. Every relationship goes through difficult times, but patience allows us to weather those storms with grace and resilience. Instead of reacting impulsively or emotionally, patience gives us the ability to listen, understand, and find solutions that work for everyone involved.

### Conclusion: Trusting the Timing of Growth

Patience is not just a virtue; it is a necessity in the growth process. Whether you're nurturing personal growth, building relationships, or pursuing professional success, patience allows you to trust the timing of growth. It gives you the space to develop, the wisdom to learn from setbacks, and the resilience to keep moving forward even when progress seems slow.

As you continue on your growth journey, remember that patience is a powerful tool. It allows you to stay grounded, to stay hopeful, and to remain committed to the process. Growth cannot be rushed, and it's only when you trust the timing of your own growth that you will experience true transformation.

Take a moment to reflect on your current growth journey. Where do you need to practice more patience? Are there areas where you're trying to rush the process instead of allowing it to unfold naturally? By cultivating patience in your life, you open the door to deeper, more meaningful growth that will last a lifetime.

**Chapter 5: Nurturing Others Through the Let Them Grow Method**

Growth is not only a personal journey; it also extends to how we support and nurture the growth of others. The Let Them Grow Method emphasizes the importance of allowing others the space and time they need to evolve. As much as we may want to guide, direct, or even rescue others, true growth comes when people are allowed to grow at their own pace. In this chapter, we will explore how to nurture the growth of others while respecting their unique paths, offering guidance without control, and supporting their personal development.

**The Importance of Supporting Others' Growth**

One of the most profound ways we can contribute to the world around us is by helping others grow. Whether it's a child, a friend, a colleague, or a partner, every person we encounter is on their own journey of growth. While we cannot control this process, we can certainly create environments that allow it to flourish. By nurturing others, we become catalysts for positive change in their lives.

Supporting others in their growth is a delicate balance. It involves offering guidance and encouragement without imposing our own expectations. True support comes from allowing others the space to explore their own strengths, weaknesses, and potential. The more we encourage others to grow on their terms, the more they can develop into their best selves. This is one of the core principles of the Let Them Grow Method.

### Creating a Supportive Environment

A critical part of nurturing others through the Let Them Grow Method is creating an environment that encourages growth. This environment should be one of safety, acceptance, and patience. When people feel supported, they are more likely to take risks, make mistakes, and ultimately grow into their full potential.

In relationships, whether personal or professional, the environment we create can either encourage or hinder growth. If someone feels pressured or judged, they may retreat or resist growth altogether. However, if they feel accepted and encouraged to explore their own ideas and paths, they are more likely to thrive.

The Let Them Grow Method encourages you to cultivate an environment that is non-judgmental and open. This means listening without interrupting, offering constructive feedback when necessary, and providing emotional support when challenges arise. It also means giving the people around you the freedom to take their own risks and make mistakes, understanding that failure is often a stepping stone to growth.

### Providing Encouragement Without Over-Interfering

It's easy to fall into the trap of trying to "fix" or "help" others in a way that undermines their growth. Often, our instinct is to jump in and offer solutions, believing that we know what's best for them. However, this approach can unintentionally stifle growth by robbing them of the opportunity to figure things out on their own.

The Let Them Grow Method teaches that encouragement is vital, but it should be balanced with the understanding that everyone must grow at their own pace. Rather than offering unsolicited advice or stepping in at the first sign of struggle, the method encourages you to support others in a more subtle, empowering way.

For example, instead of telling someone how to solve a problem, you can ask questions that prompt reflection. Instead of offering a direct solution, you can encourage them to think about the options available to them. This approach fosters independence and strengthens their problem-solving abilities.

This doesn't mean that you should remain silent or uninvolved when someone is struggling. It simply means that your role is to empower them to find their own path rather than imposing your own vision of what their growth should look like. In this way, you are nurturing their autonomy while still providing the emotional support they need.

**Balancing Patience and Encouragement**

While patience is key in allowing others to grow, encouragement plays a vital role in keeping them motivated during their journey. Finding the balance between giving people space to grow and offering them support when needed can be challenging. However, striking this balance is one of the most rewarding aspects of nurturing others.

There are times when the people around us may feel discouraged or lost, unsure of their next steps. In these moments, a few words of encouragement can make all the difference. Encouragement can remind them of their potential, reassure them that they are capable of overcoming obstacles, and inspire them to keep going.

However, encouragement should always be rooted in empathy. It's important to recognize when someone needs space and when they need support. Encouraging someone to move forward before they're ready may cause undue pressure. Conversely, withholding encouragement when someone truly needs it could lead to feelings of isolation or self-doubt.

This delicate balance is something that you can refine over time, depending on the person you're supporting and their individual needs. By being attuned to their emotional state and growth process, you can find the right moment to offer support without interfering.

### Leading by Example

One of the most powerful ways to nurture the growth of others is by leading by example. People learn a great deal from observing the behavior of those around them. If you want to inspire growth in others, you must first demonstrate the qualities that foster growth — patience, resilience, compassion, and understanding.

When you model these behaviors, you set a positive example for others to follow. If you want the people around you to be patient with their own growth, you must practice patience yourself. If you want them to trust the process of growth, you must show them that you trust it too. Your actions speak louder than your words, and when you lead by example, you encourage others to follow suit.

By embodying the principles of the Let Them Grow Method, you help create a ripple effect of positive change. Your growth becomes a source of inspiration for others, showing them that growth is possible, even when faced with challenges or setbacks. As you continue to grow yourself, you inspire others to embark on their own growth journeys.

**Respecting Individual Growth Paths**

One of the most important aspects of nurturing others is recognizing that their growth paths will look different from yours. Everyone has their own timing, their own strengths, and their own challenges. The Let Them Grow Method encourages you to respect these differences and allow others the freedom to grow in a way that feels right for them.

This means letting go of expectations about how quickly or in what direction someone should grow. Rather than comparing their progress to yours or to anyone else's, celebrate their unique journey. By doing so, you honor their individuality and empower them to make decisions that are in alignment with their values and aspirations.

**Supporting Through Challenges**

As much as we may want to shield others from hardship, challenges are an inevitable part of the growth process. The Let Them Grow Method doesn't shy away from the tough moments; instead, it teaches us to embrace them. Challenges are often where the most significant growth occurs, and it is during these times that your support can make the most profound impact.

When someone you care about faces a challenge, your role is not to remove the obstacle but to offer encouragement and guidance through it. Be there to listen, provide a safe space for them to process their feelings, and offer your unwavering belief in their ability to overcome the challenge. Your support will not only help them navigate the difficulty at hand but will also give them the strength to continue growing in the future.

**Conclusion: Empowering Others Through Growth**

Nurturing the growth of others is one of the most rewarding aspects of the Let Them Grow Method. It requires patience, empathy, and the ability to create an environment where growth can flourish. By respecting others' unique paths, offering encouragement without interference, and leading by example, you help empower those around you to reach their fullest potential.

As you continue to practice the Let Them Grow Method, remember that the act of nurturing others is a gift. By supporting their growth, you are also growing yourself. Your relationships become deeper, your understanding of others more profound, and your ability to help others flourish more impactful.

Take a moment to reflect on how you can begin nurturing the growth of others in your life. How can you provide the support they need without controlling their process? In what ways can you create an environment that encourages growth and independence? By embracing these principles, you will foster a world of growth, not only for yourself but for those around you as well.

## Chapter 6: Practical Applications: Growing Every Day

The Let Them Grow Method isn't just a philosophy or a set of abstract principles; it is a way of life that you can incorporate into your everyday actions. In this chapter, we'll explore the practical applications of the Let Them Grow Method, offering actionable steps and strategies to integrate growth into your daily routine. By consciously embracing growth every day, you cultivate a mindset that is both flexible and resilient, allowing you to live in harmony with the natural process of growth.

### The Concept of Daily Growth

Growth is not something that happens in a single moment or a series of dramatic events. It is an ongoing process that unfolds each day, sometimes in small, subtle ways, sometimes through more significant, visible changes. The Let Them Grow Method encourages us to embrace this daily evolution, recognizing that growth doesn't require perfection or immediate results. It simply requires consistency, awareness, and a willingness to learn from every experience.

Each day is an opportunity for growth, whether it's through the challenges you face, the decisions you make, or the interactions you have. Rather than waiting for a major breakthrough, begin to notice the small, everyday ways in which you are growing. This shift in perspective is essential for practicing the Let Them Grow Method because it helps you see growth in its many forms and allows you to appreciate the process rather than just the outcome.

### Embracing Small Steps Toward Growth

One of the key practical applications of the Let Them Grow Method is the idea of taking small steps. Growth doesn't need to be rushed or forced. Instead, focus on making gradual progress each day, even in small, seemingly insignificant ways. These small steps build momentum over time, creating lasting change.

For example, if you want to grow in your patience, start by practicing mindfulness in situations that usually trigger frustration. Instead of expecting instant transformation, give yourself permission to take small, manageable steps toward developing more patience. Whether it's taking deep breaths when you're feeling impatient or reminding yourself to stay present in the moment, these small actions compound and lead to significant personal growth over time.

Similarly, if you're working on your ability to let go and allow others to grow, begin by noticing moments when you're tempted to intervene or control. Instead of jumping in, practice giving the other person space. Each time you choose not to control, you are taking a step toward growth — both for yourself and the other person. These small, conscious decisions are the building blocks of a life lived in alignment with the Let Them Grow Method.

**Creating Daily Habits that Foster Growth**

Incorporating the Let Them Grow Method into your daily routine requires creating habits that support growth. Just as you would develop any new skill or habit, you must intentionally set aside time and effort to cultivate growth on a daily basis. This involves reflecting on your current habits and determining how they contribute to or hinder growth.

Start by setting aside a few minutes each day for reflection. This could be in the form of journaling, meditation, or simply sitting quietly and asking yourself questions like, "What did I learn today?" or "How did I grow in this situation?" Regular reflection allows you to assess your growth and identify areas where you can continue to improve. It also serves as a reminder to embrace the growth process, no matter how small the steps may seem.

Another practical habit is practicing gratitude. Acknowledge the progress you've made, even if it feels small or slow.

Gratitude shifts your focus from what you haven't yet achieved to what you've already accomplished, fostering a mindset of abundance and growth. Each time you express gratitude, you reinforce the belief that growth is possible and that every step forward, no matter how small, is valuable.

As you develop these habits, you'll begin to notice subtle changes in your mindset. Rather than seeing growth as a distant goal, you will come to view it as a natural, ongoing part of your everyday life.

**Setting Intentions for Growth**

Intentionality is an important aspect of the Let Them Grow Method. By setting clear intentions for your growth, you are taking an active role in shaping your path. Rather than waiting for growth to happen to you, you are proactively creating opportunities for growth.

Start by setting intentions for the areas of your life where you want to grow. This could be personal growth, professional development, or strengthening your relationships. Be specific about what you want to focus on and why it matters to you. For example, you might set an intention to practice patience more consciously in your relationships or to be more open to the idea of change in your career.

Once you've set your intentions, take small, daily actions that support them. You don't need to overhaul your entire life overnight; simply commit to making small changes that align with your goals. These small actions, when done consistently, will help you build the momentum needed for long-term growth.

Additionally, be flexible with your intentions. Life is full of unexpected twists and turns, and sometimes our growth takes us in unexpected directions. Allow yourself the freedom to adjust your intentions as you go, trusting that the process of growth will continue regardless of the specific path you take.

**Letting Go of Perfectionism**

Perfectionism can be one of the greatest obstacles to daily growth. When we hold ourselves to unrealistic standards, we create unnecessary stress and limit our ability to grow. The Let Them Grow Method encourages us to embrace imperfection and trust that growth happens even in the midst of mistakes, failures, and setbacks.

Letting go of perfectionism involves shifting your mindset from one of judgment to one of acceptance. Rather than focusing on what went wrong or what you didn't achieve, focus on the lessons you learned and how you can grow from the experience. This shift in perspective allows you to embrace your imperfections and use them as opportunities for growth.

Remember, growth is not about being perfect — it's about progress. Allow yourself to make mistakes, learn from them, and continue moving forward. By doing so, you'll create an environment where growth is encouraged and celebrated, rather than feared or avoided.

**Leveraging Challenges for Growth**

Life is full of challenges, and while they can often feel overwhelming, they are also opportunities for growth. The Let Them Grow Method teaches us to view challenges as an integral part of the growth process. Rather than avoiding difficulties, we are encouraged to face them head-on, knowing that they will help us become stronger and more resilient.

When you encounter a challenge, take a moment to reflect on what it can teach you. How can this situation contribute to your growth? What lessons can you extract from it? This mindset shift allows you to approach challenges not as roadblocks, but as stepping stones on your path to growth.

Incorporating this mindset into your daily life helps you build resilience. The more you embrace challenges as opportunities for growth, the more confident and empowered you will feel in your ability to handle whatever comes your way.

**Developing a Growth Mindset**

At the core of the Let Them Grow Method is the idea of a growth mindset. A growth mindset is the belief that abilities and intelligence can be developed through dedication, effort, and learning. This mindset is essential for embracing daily growth because it encourages you to see challenges as opportunities rather than obstacles.

To cultivate a growth mindset, begin by embracing the idea that you are always in the process of learning and evolving. Be open to feedback, seek out opportunities to learn new things, and embrace the idea that growth is a lifelong journey. The more you cultivate a growth mindset, the more easily you will navigate the ups and downs of life with grace and confidence.

**Conclusion: The Daily Commitment to Growth**

Integrating the Let Them Grow Method into your daily life requires conscious effort, but the rewards are immeasurable. By embracing small steps, creating daily habits, setting intentions, and letting go of perfectionism, you can create a life that is constantly evolving and expanding.

Remember that growth is not a destination but a journey. Every day is an opportunity to learn, evolve, and become a better version of yourself. By applying the Let Them Grow Method every day, you will cultivate a mindset of growth that empowers you to live with purpose, resilience, and peace.

## Chapter 7: Creating a Legacy of Growth for the Future

The final chapter of this workbook focuses on creating a lasting legacy of growth — not only for yourself but for the world around you. By incorporating the Let Them Grow Method into your life, you are not just experiencing personal growth in the present moment, but also contributing to the growth of others and the legacy you leave behind. The impact of this method can extend far beyond your own life, creating a ripple effect that influences future generations.

### The Power of Legacy

When we think of legacy, we often think of something grand — monumental achievements or lasting accomplishments that are remembered by future generations. However, legacy is more than just what you leave behind in terms of tangible results or material possessions. The true power of legacy lies in the way you impact others, the values you instill, and the lessons you teach.

Your legacy is built upon the principles you embody, the choices you make, and the way you interact with others. By living in alignment with the Let Them Grow Method, you are creating a legacy of growth, compassion, and empowerment. This type of legacy is not just about the success you achieve, but about the positive influence you have on the lives of others.

**Teaching Growth to Others**

One of the most powerful ways to create a legacy of growth is by teaching others the Let Them Grow Method. Whether you are mentoring a colleague, guiding a child, or supporting a friend, you can share the principles of this method to help others embrace growth in their own lives.

By teaching others to let go of control and allow room for growth, you are passing on a valuable lesson that will help them navigate life with greater ease and confidence. Your example of embracing growth and letting others grow will inspire those around you to do the same. This cycle of teaching and learning creates a ripple effect, spreading the Let Them Grow Method to new generations and diverse communities.

Start by sharing your journey with others. Tell your friends and family about the Let Them Grow Method and how it has impacted your life. Offer support and guidance to others who are also striving to grow. Through conversations, mentorship, and shared experiences, you can help others incorporate this approach into their own lives, creating a legacy of growth that extends far beyond your own experience.

**Cultivating Growth in Communities**

The Let Them Grow Method isn't just about individual growth — it is about creating environments where growth is encouraged, nurtured, and supported. This can happen within your family, your workplace, your community, and even your wider social network. By fostering a culture of growth, you contribute to creating spaces where others feel empowered to develop and thrive.

Start by being intentional about the way you interact with others. Create an environment where people feel safe to express themselves, make mistakes, and learn from their experiences. Encourage open communication, active listening, and patience. Celebrate the growth of others as much as you celebrate your own. When you acknowledge and nurture the growth of those around you, you create a culture of growth that will continue to flourish.

In your community or workplace, look for ways to support others' growth. Whether it's through offering mentorship, providing resources, or simply offering encouragement, you can contribute to the collective growth of those around you. A community built on growth is one where everyone has the opportunity to reach their full potential, and where the Let Them Grow Method can thrive.

**The Legacy of Patience and Trust**

At the heart of the Let Them Grow Method is patience — the patience to let go and trust in the process of growth, both for yourself and for others. By embracing this principle, you create a legacy of trust, not just in others, but in the natural process of life itself.

Trusting the process of growth means believing that, even when things are uncertain or challenging, everything is unfolding as it should. This mindset encourages resilience, allowing you to face obstacles with the confidence that they are part of your growth journey. It also encourages others to trust themselves and the process of their own development.

By embodying patience and trust, you teach others to do the same. You show them that growth takes time, that setbacks are a natural part of the process, and that progress doesn't always look like what we expect. When you pass on the legacy of patience and trust, you are empowering others to cultivate the same qualities in their own lives, creating a ripple effect that extends far beyond your immediate circle.

**Creating Lasting Change Through Growth**

One of the most powerful aspects of the Let Them Grow Method is its ability to create lasting change. Unlike quick fixes or superficial changes, growth is a process that unfolds over time, resulting in deep, meaningful transformations. By committing to growth, you are not only changing your own life but also contributing to a broader cultural shift — one that values patience, trust, and the freedom to grow at your own pace.

As you continue to practice the Let Them Grow Method, you will notice subtle, yet profound changes in your life. You may find that you are more patient, more open-minded, and more compassionate. You may find that your relationships are stronger, that you are more resilient in the face of challenges, and that you experience greater fulfillment and peace.

These changes, though gradual, create a foundation for lasting transformation. The more you embrace growth, the more you inspire others to do the same. In this way, the Let Them Grow Method becomes a tool for creating lasting change in your life, in your relationships, and in your community. Through growth, you have the power to leave a positive and lasting legacy.

**Reflecting on Your Growth Journey**

As you reflect on the legacy of growth that you are creating, take a moment to appreciate how far you've come. Acknowledge the progress you've made, the lessons you've learned, and the growth you've experienced. Remember that growth is not always about the destination — it's about the journey.

Think about the ways in which you have already impacted others through your growth. How have your actions, your mindset, and your example influenced those around you? Reflect on the relationships you have nurtured, the support you have offered, and the positive changes you have inspired.

Consider the legacy you want to leave behind. What values do you want to pass on to future generations? How do you want others to remember you? By living in alignment with the Let Them Grow Method, you are already creating a legacy of growth, compassion, and empowerment. The more you embody these principles, the greater the impact you will have on the world around you.

### Conclusion: The Lasting Power of Growth

As we conclude this workbook, remember that the Let Them Grow Method is not just a set of principles to follow; it is a way of living that has the power to transform your life and the lives of those around you. By embracing growth, trusting the process, and supporting others on their journey, you are creating a legacy that will extend far beyond your own lifetime.

Continue to practice the Let Them Grow Method every day, knowing that the impact of your growth will ripple outwards, creating positive change in the world. Your legacy of growth will inspire future generations to live with patience, trust, and the freedom to grow at their own pace. Through your commitment to growth, you are creating a lasting legacy that will continue to flourish long after you are gone.

Made in the USA
Middletown, DE
09 January 2025

69138612R00040